Australia's Neighbours

India

DISCOVER THE COUNTRY, CULTURE AND PEOPLE

Jane Hinchey

REDBACK publishing

First published 2019 by
Redback Publishing
PO Box 357 Frenchs Forest NSW 2086
Australia

www.redbackpublishing.com.au
orders@redbackpublishing.com.au

Reprinted 2023

ISBN 978-1925860-65-8 PBK

Author: Jane Hinchey
Editor: Caroline Thomas
Designer: Redback Publishing

Original illustrations © Redback Publishing 2023
Originated by Redback Publishing

Printed and bound in Malaysia

Acknowledgements
Abbreviations: l—left, r—right, b—bottom, t—top, c—centre, m—middle
We would like to thank the following for permission to reproduce photographs: (Images © shutterstock)

NATIONAL LIBRARY OF AUSTRALIA
A catalogue record for this book is available from the National Library of Australia

Contents

Map of India

Government

India is a federal parliamentary democratic republic. India's government is divided into three parts: the legislative, executive and judiciary. The President of India is the Head of State. The Prime Minister of India is responsible for running the federal government. The President of India is elected for five years. The President can choose the Prime Minister.

India is made up of 29 states and 7 territories, each with its own government.

Snapshot

Official name:	Republic of India
Population:	1,628,769,962,768 (September 2022)
Capital:	New Delhi
Land area:	2,973,190 square kilometres
Official languages:	Hindi, English
Religions:	Hinduism, Islam, Buddhism, Christianity, Sikhism, Jainism
System of Government:	Federal parliamentary democratic republic
Currency:	Indian rupee

Major Sites

- Taj Mahal
- The Ganges
- Amer Fort
- The Red Fort
- Golden Temple
- New Delhi
- Mumbai
- Jaipur
- Himachal Pradesh
- Goa

Fun Facts

- India has the second largest English speaking population in the world, with 125 million English speakers.
- Chess was invented in India.
- India boasts the highest cricket ground in the world. The Chail Cricket Ground in Chail, Himachal Pradesh, is located at an altitude of 2,444 meters.

Meet India

India is the world's largest democracy, with the second largest population in the world.

India is the seventh largest country in the world. It is a land of contrasts. Each region has distinct landforms, vegetation and climate. It boasts some of the world's most beautiful scenery, from soaring mountains and high plateaux to vast deserts and low-lying plains and rivers.

India is a peninsula, surrounded on three sides by water. In the west is the Arabian Sea, in the south is the Indian Ocean, and in the east is the Bay of Bengal. It shares borders with Pakistan, Bangladesh, Myanmar, China, Bhutan, and Nepal. It also shares a border with Afghanistan through Kashmir, which is not internationally recognised.

India has a number of different climates. In the South, the climate is tropical, and gets very hot in summer and cooler in winter. The western deserts are hot and dry. Northern India is sub-tropical, while its mountainous regions have alpine climates. The Himalayas get extremely cold. India gets monsoon rain that sweeps across the country for three months of the year.

There are 22 official languages in India, but no national language. There are also over 1,600 different dialects, and 29 Indian languages with over a million speakers. English is widely spoken and used for business and government. In 2018, data from the 2011 census was finally released, showing Hindi as the most widely spoken language, with 44% of the population speaking it as a first language.

Learn The Lingo

Hello:	Namaste
Goodbye:	Alavida
Yes:	Haan
No:	Nahin
Please:	Krpya
Thank you:	Dhanyavad

At a Glance

Economy

India's economy is booming, growing by 7.7% in the first quarter of 2018.

Main Agriculture:

India ranks second in the world for its farm output. It is the world's largest producer of pulses, rice, wheat, spices and spice products. India is the second largest fruit producer in the world.

Main Exports:

India is the 17th largest export economy in the world. Exports include refined petroleum, diamonds, packaged medicines, jewellery and cars. Main export partners are the USA, the UAE, Hong Kong, China and the UK.

Main Imports:

India's top imports include crude Petroleum, gold, diamonds, coal briquettes and telephones. Main import partners are China, the USA, the UAE, Saudi Arabia and Switzerland.

Natural Resources:

India has the fourth-largest reserves of coal in the world. Other natural resources include natural gas, chromite, iron ore, manganese, mica, limestone, bauxite, rare earth elements, titanium ore, diamonds, petroleum, and arable land.

Daily Life

Fast Fact!
Three of the world's major religions, Buddhism, Hinduism and Sikhism began in India.

India is the second most populated country in the world. In 2018 the population exceeded 1.35 billion. India is made up of many different ethnic groups. The country is divided into 29 different states and 7 union territories. Each state has its own traditions, language, and costumes, but ethnic groups, customs and language can even vary from village to village.

Family Life

Family is the focus of daily life in India. Families are large and it is common to live with two or more generations, especially in rural areas where many generations help run farms. In cities, grandparents help care for young children, so their parents can work.

Families are patriarchal, meaning the head of the family is male and makes all major decisions, including what career paths the children will take and who they will marry. Most marriages are arranged by the bride and groom's family, sometimes with the support of a professional matchmaker. Women are expected to obey their husbands, while children are taught to respect their elders.

Mutigenerational Joint Families

Hindus have mutigenerational joint families, officially called a Hindu Undivided Family (HUF). The family is made up of relatives that share a common ancestor, and the wives of the men in that family. Once a woman marries, she joins her husband's HUF. This joint family structure has also been adopted by many non-Hindus out of economic necessity as the family provides for every member, and the Indian government recognises the HUF as a legal entity. However stricter Muslim families segregate men from women, so this arrangement doesn't work.

Critics of the mutigenerational joint family point to many inequalities of the system, including the unfair division of inheritances. Female members of the family are usually at a disadvantage, and it is common for daughter-in laws to be forced to work as servants for their new family.

Hindu Caste System

India's Caste System

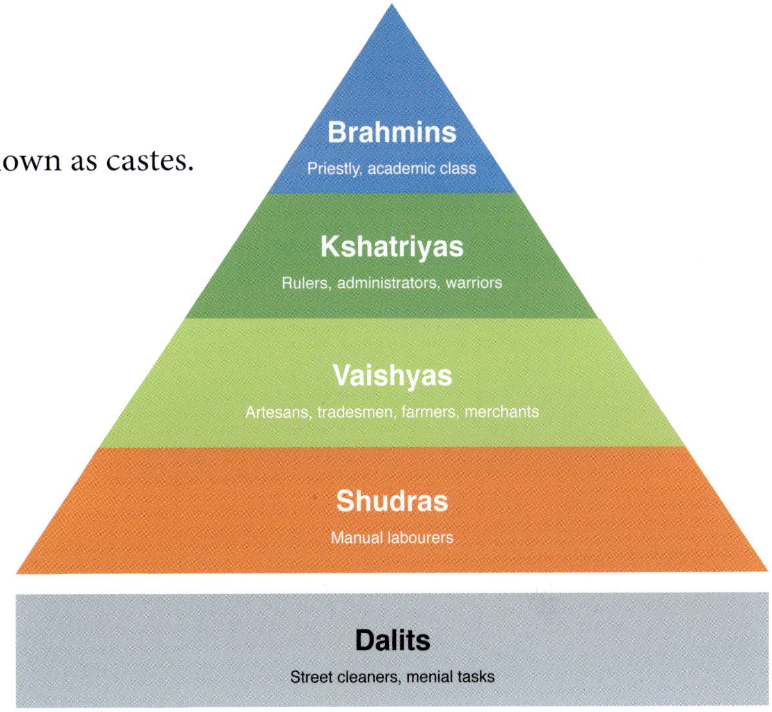

Hindu people are born into social groups, known as castes. The caste system has four main categories:

- Brahmins
- Kshatriyas
- Vaishyas
- Shudras

These four main castes are further divided into about 3,000 castes and 25,000 sub-castes, each based on their specific occupation.
Outside of the Hindu caste system are the Dalits, also known as the untouchables. The untouchables have always been considered the lowest in society.

Dalits had no rights, and it was impossible to rise above this social ranking. Since 1950, the Indian Constitution has forbidden discrimination and now India's Dalits receive some government support. However the division between the Dalits and the rest of society remains strong. In recent years there have been violent protests with Dalits demanding changes to the systems that oppress them.

While the caste system is Hindu, all Indians, irrespective of religion, are somewhat influenced by the system. Some progress towards equality has been made, but caste identities remain strong. Surnames are almost always an indication of what caste a person belongs to.

Education

Children in India attend primary school from age 6 to 11. High school caters for students up to age 17. About 10% of children don't attend school, with the majority of these coming from poor families. For children from wealthier families, there is a lot of pressure to do well in school. The Indian government provides free education to girls over 14 years in a bid to keep them in school.

After school, many Indians attend technical college or university. India has the third largest higher education system, after China and the USA. There are around 890 universities in India.

Did You Know?

There is a school being built in Chennai, India that prioritises happiness over academics and grades. Students will work on projects that look for solutions to real-world issues, as well as focus on subjects they enjoy, and personal development areas. The school wants to focus on students becoming happy and compassionate people.

The Sari

A variety of traditional clothes have developed over time in India, all influenced by region, culture, religion and climate. The most famous of India's traditional outfits is the sari. Worn by women, a sari is a piece of cloth that is draped over the body in various styles. They range from simple fabrics to ornate silks for important occasions.

Sports

India is a nation that takes sport very seriously. While hockey is the official national sport, cricket is the country's most popular sport. All over India, in every city and every village, people play cricket. Introduced to India by the British during colonial times, cricket players are treated like rock stars. There are many cricket stadiums around the country. Poorer people will watch games on television. Even those people who don't have their own television will find one nearby for important matches.

Other popular sports include polo, tennis and soccer.

Sachin Tendulkar, India's God of Cricket

Sachin Ramesh Tendulkar is a former international cricketer and a former captain of the Indian national team. He is the highest run scorer of all time in International cricket, regarded as one of the greatest batsmen of all time. Admired all around the cricket world, he is elevated to god-like status is India.

system. India's constitution guarantees free healthcare for all its citizens, however those who can afford it, pay out of pocket to access private healthcare.

Public healthcare is especially poor in rural areas. There are 1.4 million doctors in India and yet there is a shortage of experienced doctors in rural areas.

Preventable Diseases

It is estimated that 2 million children under the age of 5 die annually of diseases such as malaria, measles, pneumonia, typhoid and diarrhoea.

Girl Power

A 30-year-old Air India pilot became the world's youngest female captain of a Boeing 777 when she flew the world's largest twin jet during advanced training in London.

Women

Under the Constitution of India women have the right to equality, dignity, and freedom from discrimination, however the reality is quite different and women in India continue to face numerous problems including gender inequality. The role of women has progressed in modern India but still differs depending on social status. At home, there is a lot of pressure to marry, and child rearing still falls primarily to women.

There is pressure on many women to produce a male heir. Violence against women is endemic. In some areas, women are often accused of witchcraft and killed. Over 70% of Indian women experience domestic violence. The Criminal Law Act provides a legal framework to deal with this, although it is rare that a woman will pursue it. Culturally, domestic violence is seen as a private family matter.

Over the past 25 years there has been a decline in women working. For those women that do work, the gender pay gap is as high as 27%. In 2018, new laws were passed to improve maternity benefits for women in India's workforce and encourage them to further their careers.

Despite the hurdles women face, India has one of the highest number of female politicians in the world. Women have held high offices in India including that of the President and Prime Minister.

Religion

Religion is the foundation of India's culture and daily life. India is the birthplace of Buddhism, Hinduism, Sikhism and Jainism. Hinduism is the most widely practised religion, making up about 80% of the population.

India is a secular state and all religions are given equal status by law. There are some religious tensions between Hindus and Muslims, and Hindus and Christians, but generally Indian people are tolerant of the different faiths.

Hinduism

Hinduism developed around 4,000 years ago. There is no single founder, and no specific set of teachings. While there is believed to be a single supreme being, followers worship many deities, or gods.

Popular Hindu deities include:

- Brahma: The first of three gods in the Hindu Trinity. He is believed to be the creator of everything in the universe.
- Ganesha: This beloved deity has the head of an elephant. Hindus consider him the Remover of Obstacles, and ask for his assistance on all matters in life.
- Lakshmi: This is the goddess of good fortune, wealth, and well-being.
- Hanuman: Known as the monkey king, he is featured in the great Hindu epic the Ramayana. Hanuman is worshipped for his unyielding devotion to Rama and is remembered for his selfless dedication.

Islam

Islam is the second most common religion in India. Muslims believe in one god, called Allah, who gave his message to a prophet called Mohammed. The holy book is called the Koran.

Ramadan

Ramadan is the most important event on the Islamic calendar. Ramadan is a month of fasting during daylight hours to display faith to Allah. At the end of Ramadan, there is a big three-day celebration where families and friends celebrate together, called Eid al-Fitr, or the festival of breaking the fast.

In the fifth century BC, a prince called Siddhartha Guatama turned his back on his life of privilege and went on a spiritual journey. This led to the birth of one of the world's great religions, Buddhism. Despite being founded in India, and being embraced all around the world, the Buddhist population of India is relatively small. There are about 7 million Buddhists, although this number has grown, with many Dalits renouncing Hinduism because of the caste system, and instead embracing the tenets of Buddhism.

Ullambana is the main Buddhist festival. Buddhists believe the gates of hell open on this day, making it easy for the dead to visit their loved ones. It is celebrated on the 15th day of the 7th month of the lunar calendar.

Sikhism

The Sikh religion began around 600 years ago, and today has around 20 million followers worldwide. Sikhs believe in one god, reincarnation and that everyone is equal. When a Sikh man has devoted himself to his religion, there are five symbols that he will carry or wear.

The five Ks are: Kesh (uncut hair)
Kara (a steel bracelet) Kanga (a wooden comb)
Kaccha (cotton underwear)
Kirpan (steel sword)

Sacred Cows

Cows are considered to be sacred, so Hindus don't eat beef. It is not uncommon to see cows wandering the streets in India.

Jainism

Jains believe they must live a pure life. To do so they practice:

- Non-violence
- Truth
- Non-stealing
- Chastity
- Non-attachment

Life in Cities

India has 46 cities with a population of more than one million people. Mumbai, Delhi and Kolkata and their outer regions are known as mega cities.

India's cities are noisy, polluted and densely populated. But they also have world-class facilities, restaurants and shopping centres, and life for the more fortunate can be exciting and cosmopolitan. The wealthy live in gated seclusion, in beautiful homes, and employ servants and drivers. India has a growing middle class and these families also live in comfort, with hired help. Others live in high-rise apartments, in new residential areas. Those with the money have access to great galleries, theatre and music performances, films, public events and exhibits. Their children have the opportunity to be well-educated and have good careers.

City Slums

India's economy is booming, and yet 100 million of its residents live in urban slums. Many of the residents work for India's wealthy families. The streets are narrow and often sewage water runs into open drains. Some areas lack basic sanitation services, and often have no access to electricity or clean water. Child labour is common in these slums. However some slum dwellers are advocates for the community, and many people now buy their own homes. These inhabitants look for street lighting and sewerage facilities, and generally work to make their communities safer.

However many people live in poverty. They migrate to the city from rural areas looking for work, but India's cities are ill prepared for the numbers. Basic infrastructure like water supply, electricity lines and roads cannot cope with the constant rise in numbers. More often than not these new residents find themselves struggling and living in the ever-expanding slum areas.

Life in Rural Areas

Over 72% of India's population still lives in towns and villages, or in the countryside. There are over 50,000 villages in India. Life in the countryside can be tough, but community oriented. Some places are difficult to get to, so relationships with neighbours are important. How difficult life is, depends on whether you're rich or poor and what caste you were born into. Wealthy people in the countryside live in two storey houses, with running water, electricity and servants, but the majority of rural dwellers live in small mud or straw shacks. These villagers often have to walk miles each day to access clean drinking water. People bathe in nearby creeks or streams.

Over half of India's population is employed in farming. Fishing is also a major industry. Although agriculture is one of the country's most important industries, life is tough for farmers. Many farmers still till the land by hand. Very few of them can afford modern farm equipment, and only about half of them have irrigation systems.

Education is often seen as a luxury

Children drop out of school early to help on their family farms. Other infrastructure, such as roads and access to health care, is limited.

The Arts

Indian culture stretches back thousands of years, with rich art forms developing over that time. The first sculptures in India date back to the Indus Valley civilization 5,000 years ago. The arrival of religions such as Hinduism, Buddhism and Jainism further influenced art forms. Today, music, theatre, art and literature are enjoyed as much as ever, but the most popular of all the art forms is film.

Great Tales

Indian people love a grand tale. India's history is awash with famous stories of revenge, war and most importantly, love. The earliest works of literature were epics, long poems, travelogues, plays, and verse. The two most famous epics are the Mahabharata and the Ramayana.

Music and Dance

Music and dance have developed from using traditional instruments and epic tales, to today's modern styles of both, influenced by the USA.

Classical dances are often regional and based on India's myths and folk tales. There are many different traditional dance styles, such as Bharatanatyam, Kathak, Kathakali, Manipuri, and Odissi, but all use very specific hand movements called mudras.

Classical music is separated into two major traditions: Hindustani music of North India and Carnatic music of South India. Different regions also have their own traditional music forms.

Traditional Instruments

Sitar: Probably India's most well known traditional instrument, the sita is similar to a guitar.
Kamanche: One of the world's earliest known bowed instruments.
Tambura: A string instrument that is plucked.
Tabla: Two drums of different sizes, played by one performer.

Folk Art

Folk art has survived in many parts of the country by being passed from generation to generation. Many folk art forms depict religious epics or Gods and Goddesses, and are influenced by the region they're from. For example Phad is a type of religious scroll originating in Rajasthan. The paintings are done in vegetable colours and portray folk deities.

Quite different in style are Gond, painted by the Gondi tribe in Madhya Pradesh. These paintings depict flora and fauna in bold colours. Traditionally Gond were created using charcoal, cow dung, leaves and coloured soil, but today artists use acrylic paints.

Bollywood

Three Great Bollywood Films for Kids

Rockford: a film about schoolchildren and their struggles.
Taare Zameen Par: an inspiring film about a dyslexic boy.
Jajantaram Mamantaram: a film inspired by Gulliver's Travels.

India's film industry, known as Bollywood, is the largest in the world. Bollywood studios produce over 1,000 films year. India is the leading film market in the world. In 2016, 2.2 billion movie tickets were sold in India, twice the amount of China in second place. About 14 million people go to the cinema every day. Bollywood films are produced in numerous languages, including Hindi, Gujarati, Punjabi, Malayalam, Assamese, Bengali and Telugu.

Bollywood films involve a lot of drama, action and romance. Another key component is song and dance. Dance numbers are especially important between the hero and heroine. The dance-form used in films is a mixture of styles such as Indian folk dance, belly dancing and modern dance. Bollywood dance styles have become famous around the world.

There are many famous actors, but the undisputable King of Bollywood is Shah Rukh Khan. In India he is known as King Khan, or SRK. He has starred in over 80 films and in terms of income and creative output, is one of the most successful actors in the world.

History of Bollywood

A number of short films were made in the late 1800s by French filmmakers, The Lumiere brothers, but the first film produced by an Indian filmmaker was Raja Harishchandra, released in 1913.

History

One of the world's oldest civilisations was in India. The Indus Valley Civilisation began in north-west India around 2,600 BC. Indus Valley cities were well-planned and very advanced, and included plumbing, trade routes and innovative agriculture methods. Between 1,500 and 1,200 BC the Aryans migrated to the area, bringing with them stories that eventually became the Vedas, which formed the basis of Hinduism.

Ashoka and the Mauryan Empire

Ashoka the Great was emperor of the Maurya Dynasty who ruled the Indian subcontinent from 269 BC to 232 BC. Known to be a cruel leader, he had a complete change of character after viewing the bodies his army had left on a battlefield. He converted to Buddhism and ruled using the key tenets of love, peace and kindness. He promoted vegetarianism, and the unnecessary slaughter of animals was abolished. He built many hospitals and universities, and treated his subjects as equals, regardless of their religion, politics and caste.

Mughal Empire

In 711, Muslims from Central Asia settled near the mouth of the Indus River and over the next several centuries, moved south and conquered land on the subcontinent. The Mughal Empire was founded in 1526 by Babur, a descendant of Genghis Khan. Babur and the successive Mughal rulers built great cities and oversaw important works of art, such as the Taj Mahal.

The British ruled the Indian subcontinent from the late 18th century until 1947, when India's independence movement succeeded. A key leader of India's independence movement was Mohandas Gandhi. Gandhi used non-violent methods to protest against British rule. His efforts earned him the title Mahatma, which means "great soul."

As the British quit colonial India, they partitioned the country based on religion. Over the next two decades, approximately nine million Hindus and Sikhs moved into India and five million Muslims moved to Pakistan. It was one of the largest forced migrations in history and left an estimated one million people dead.

- **End of British rule. The partition of the subcontinent into Hindu India and the Muslim-majority state of Pakistan.**
- **Widespread communal bloodshed after partition. Hundreds of thousands die.**
- **Mahatma Gandhi assassinated by a Hindu extremist.**
  War with Pakistan over disputed territory of Kashmir.
- **A new Indian Constitution was ratified.**

A Great Stateswoman

Indira Gandhi was Prime Minister from 19 January 1966 to 24 March 1977, and again from 14 January 1980 until her assassination on 31 October 1984.
She is credited with the nationalisation of banks, liberation of Bangladesh and 20 point programme for the upliftment of the poor.

She was the daughter of India's first Prime Minister, Jawaharlal Nehru, and the mother of another Prime Minister, Rajiv Gandhi. Indira Gandhi was one of India's most remarkable political leaders after independence.

Indian Food

Indian food is so common in the west that it can be surprising just how diverse it is. Indian cuisine has developed over time and is influenced by geography, weather, access to ingredients and ethnic groups. The country's main religions also employ different dietary restrictions.

Southern Indian food is hot and eaten with chillies and rice, while northern cuisine is less spicy and served with flat bread such as parathas and chapattis. Most regions use an array of spices. Staples include lentils, chickpeas, rice, yoghurt, onion, garlic and turmeric, aromatic herbs and spices and ghee.

Mealtime

Most people eat a morning meal, lunch and an evening meal. The most important meal of the day is dinner, which families eat together. Numerous dishes are served, from which you help yourself. Meals usually comprise of rice, chapati, meat, vegetable and lentil dishes, salad, yogurt, and pickles. While people do use cutlery, it is also common to eat using your fingers.

Quench Your Thirst

Popular drinks in India include tea and the yoghurt drink, lassi.

Etiquette Alert!

Do not use your left hand to eat! Indians consider the left hand to be unclean. (It's the hand they use when they go to the toilet.) This probably makes life difficult for people who are naturally left-handed.

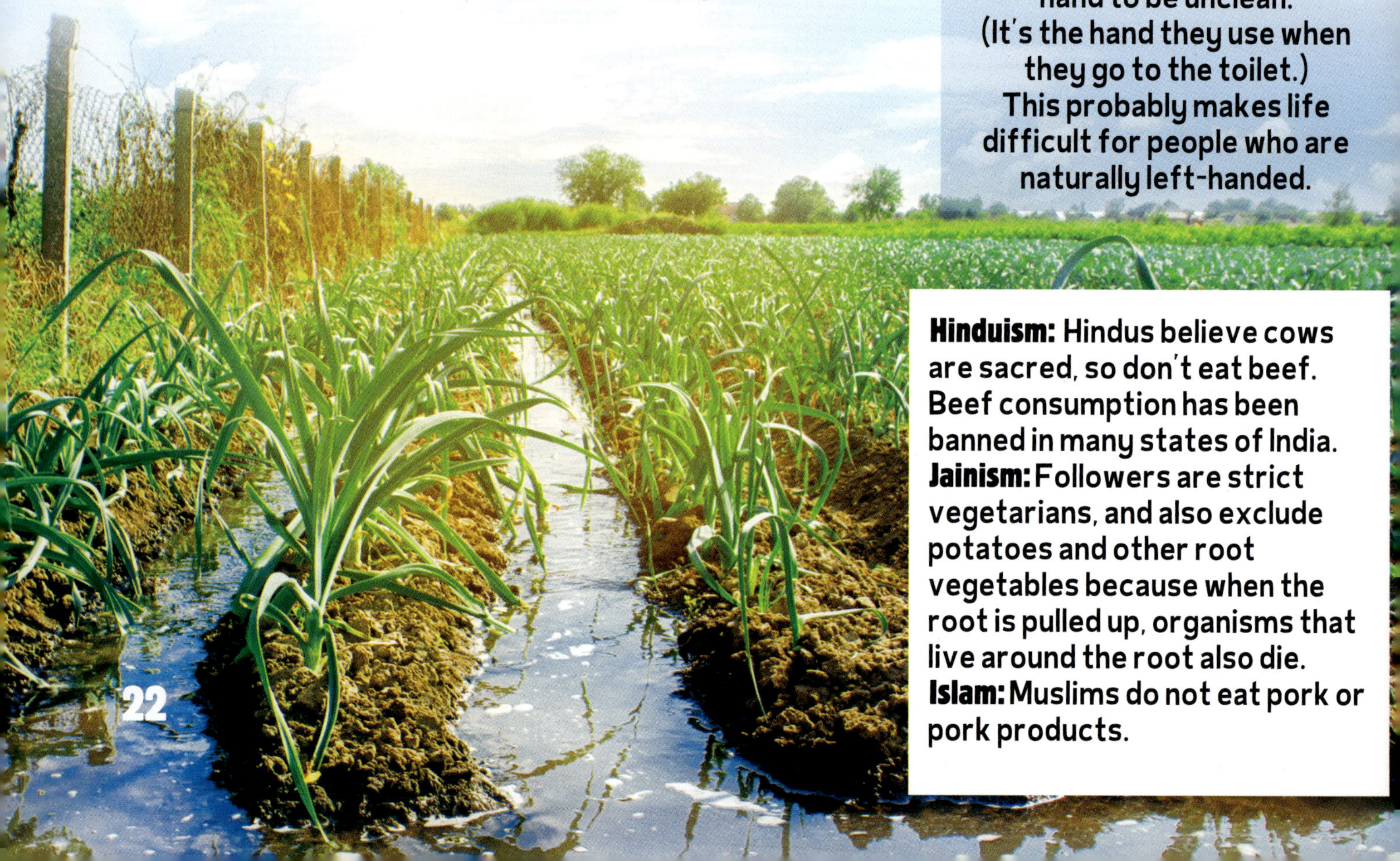

Hinduism: Hindus believe cows are sacred, so don't eat beef. Beef consumption has been banned in many states of India.
Jainism: Followers are strict vegetarians, and also exclude potatoes and other root vegetables because when the root is pulled up, organisms that live around the root also die.
Islam: Muslims do not eat pork or pork products.

On the Menu

Dishes from Northern India

Aloo gobi

Sautéed cauliflower and potatoes, with garam masala, turmeric and curry leaves.

Chicken Tikka Masala

Chicken marinated in a yogurt tomato sauce.

Daal

A popular lentil and spice dish.

Naan Rotti

A baked soft flatbread.

Palek Paneer

Pieces of paneer in a spinach curry.

Samosa

Potatoes, onions, peas, coriander, and lentils in pastry triangles.

Tandoori Chicken

Marinated, roasted chicken with spices and yoghurt.

Dishes from Southern India

Dosa

A type of savoury pancake.

Papadams

Thin deep fried flour, lentil or chickpea starter.

Kuzhakkattai

Vegetarian sweet dumplings.

Vada

Savory snack made from lentil and gram flour, often eaten with chutney.

Geography and Climate

Mountain Ranges

Northern India is mountainous, with eight important mountain ranges. The most famous mountain range in India is the Himalayas, which run across the top of India and into Nepal and China. The mountains are covered in snow, and there are farmlands in the valleys.

Southern India is home to two mountain ranges — the Western and Eastern Ghats, which border the plateau heartland.

Indo-Gangetic Plain

The Indo-Gangetic Plain is a 2.5 million kilometre rich, fertile area encompassing most of northern and eastern India. The area is named after the Ganges River and the Indus River, two of the extensive river systems that weave across this region. Many of India's ancient empires grew out of this region, including the Indus Valley Civilisation. Now, many of India's largest cities are located in the region, including New Delhi, Kolkata, Jaipur, and Varanasi. It is one of the most intensely farmed regions in the world.

Desert Region

The Thar Desert, also known as the Great Indian Desert, covers an area of 200,000 square kilometres between India and Pakistan. More than 60% of the desert lies in the state of Rajasthan, home to some of India's most famous cities and historical sites. The desert is covered with shifting sand dunes, and salt lakes that fill during monsoon season.

The Great Ganges

The revered Ganges River rises in the Himalayas and flows 3,877 kilometres east to the Bay of Bengal. Human development has replaced all the original natural vegetation. The Ganges supports one of the world's highest densities of humans on earth.

India's rich flora habitats range from deciduous forests and thick tropical jungles to cool temperate woods. There are tropical forests in the east and pine and coniferous woodlands in the western Himalayas. The Himalayan foothills are home to deciduous trees and shrubs, bamboos, fern and grass, while the Indo-Gangetic plain provides a diverse range of habitats. These are all home to a rich variety of creatures.

While much of India's natural world has been destroyed during the country's rapid development, there is a growing trend towards environmentalism to maintain and save what's left. To protect wildlife, India now has 104 national parks covering an area of 40,501 square kilometres.

There are over 500 species of mammals in India, 200 species of birds and over 30,000 species of insects. Animals such as the Asian elephant, lion, Royal Bengal Tiger, and Indian Bison all call India home, as well as numerous species of leopards, deer and monkey.

Some of India's exotic animals are close to extinction, including:

- Greater One-Horned Rhinoceros
- Nilgiri Tahr
- Bengal Tigers
- Asiatic Lion
- Black Buck

Tourism and Major Sites

India is a vast country with a rich history, so has much to offer visitors. Tourism is booming, with over 10 million visitors in 2017.

Varanasi and the Ganges

Varanasi is one of the oldest continuously inhabited cities in the world, and sacred to Hindus, Buddhists and Jains. It is a centre for all areas of the arts, and famous for it's silks and brocades. Located on the Ganges River, pilgrims descend upon its sacred waters at dawn to cleanse their sufferings and wash their sins away.

Ellora Caves

Ellora Caves is a large monastery-temple cave cut from rock. Constructed between the seventh and ninth centuries, the caves are devoted to Hindu, Buddhist and Jainism deities. There are 100 caves, although only 34 are open to the public. Listed as a World Heritage site, it is truly one of the country's ancient wonders.

Kerala Backwaters

Peaceful stretches of canals, lakes and lagoons stretch 900-kilometres through the southern Indian state of Kerala. Visitors explore the states stunning natural beauty by boat, a calm respite after some of India's more hectic tourist destinations.

Delhi

India's capital is a massive mega city, but in the centre of it all is the historical heart of the city, Old Delhi, filled with important historical sites. Some of those include:

- The Red Fort: A 17th-century Mughal fortress built in towering red sandstone.
- India Gate: Commemorating the Indian soldiers killed in the First World War.
- Humayan's Tomb: A red-sandstone tomb of Mughal Emperor Humayun, built in 1572.
- Qutb Minar: A tower built in 1193 after the defeat of Delhi's last Hindu kingdom.
- Old Delhi: Once a walled city, it is the most historic part of the metropolis, dating back to the time of the Moghuls.

Taj Mahal

India's most famous tourist attraction, and its beloved crown jewel is the Taj Mahal - One of the 7 New Wonders of the World

The Taj Mahal is a mausoleum of white marble in Agra, Uttar Pradesh. Ruler of the Mughal Empire, Shah Jahan, had the mausoleum constructed to honour his favourite wife, Mumtaz Mahal, after her death in 1631.

Taj Mahal literally means 'the crown of palaces'. Over 22,000 labourers and 1,000 elephants worked for 22 years to complete it. Masons, inlayers, carvers, painters, and other artisans were brought from as far away as Iran to work on it. A total of 43 different precious and semi precious stones were used to decorate it. It is one of the most beautiful buildings in the world, and India's top tourist attraction.

Pushkar Camel Fair

Held annually in November, the Pushkar Camel Fair is one of India's most popular and epic events. Thousands of camels, horses and cattle, and over 400,000 people congregate in the Rajasthan desert, for two weeks of livestock fairs and cultural events.

Important Sites

As of June 2018, India has 37 UNESCO World Heritage sites, the sixth most of any country. Many of these make up the country's most important tourist destinations.

- 29 World Cultural Heritage Sites
- 7 World Natural Heritage Sites
- 1 Mixed sites (Cultural and Natural)

Transport

India is a large country with a huge population and diverse geography. While the country has developed economically, and improvements to transport infrastructure have been made, there is still a long way to go. India's road network needs major improvement and is congested. Its transport systems are out-dated and crowded. Most people ride bicycles or walk, or use the country's crowded public transport system. India's public transport system is one of the most heavily used systems in the world. Another popular mode of transport for shorter journeys is human-pulled or motorised rickshaws.

Road

India's road network of 4.87 million km is the second largest in the world, with early roads being traced back to 2,800 BC and the Indus Valley Civilisation.

While many rural areas still struggle with no or minimal infrastructure, India's major cities and urban areas have expressways and highways. Car ownership has risen and India is now the fourth largest automobile market in the world. However, congested roads and financial concerns mean many Indian people will continue to ride bikes or catch tuk tuks.

Railways

First built during British rule, India's rail network is now the most heavily used system on the planet. Every day over 20,000 trains carry 3 million tonne of goods and over 23 million people across vast distances.

Did You Know?

Indian Railway employs 1.3 million people, making it the single largest employer on the planet. In 2018, 13,000 employees who had been on unauthorised leave were sacked at one time.

Railway Snapshot

Tracks: 108,706 km
Daily passenger trains: 12,617
Passenger numbers: 23 Million daily
Daily freight trains: 7,421
Daily freight: 3 million tonnes
Stations: 7,172 stations

Water Transport

India has a 7,500 kilometre long coastline with approximately 14,500 kilometres of navigable waterways, but travel by boat is still underutilised. Moving freight by boat is common in Goa, Kerala, Assam and West Bengal, but underused elsewhere.

Inland Waterways Authority of India (IWAI) is developing 18 new ferry terminals in six cities. All the cities are located on the 'National Waterway 1', the longest waterway in India. The 1,620 km long waterway runs from Haldia in Sagar to Allahabad.

India has a large shipping fleet, although it is in dire need of modernising, with over 40% of ships over 20-years old.

Air Transport

India is the world's fastest growing domestic aviation market. Cheaper airfares and a growing middle class means that more people than ever are choosing to fly domestically, as well as overseas. There are 335 airports in India, including 11 international airports. The Indira Gandhi International Airport is the main international airport situated in New Delhi. Air India is the country's national airline and the third largest airline on the domestic air passenger market.

In 2017, 265 million passengers passed through Indian airports, with that number predicted to rise to nearly 300 million in 2018.

Fun Fact

India's first solar ferry started operation between Vaikkom and Thavanakkadavu in the Indian state of Keralaon 12 January 2017.

Flags, Symbols and Emblems

Flag of India

India’s flag has three horizontal colours in equal proportion. The colours are deep saffron on the top, white in the middle and dark green at the bottom.

Deep saffron represents courage and sacrifice. White stands for peace, unity and truth.
Green symbolises faith and fertility.

In the centre of the flag is a blue wheel called the Dharma Chakra, or “Wheel of Law” The Dharma Chakra represents the progress of the nation and the importance of justice. The blue represents the sky and the ocean.

The flag was adopted on 22 July 1947, after India became independent from Great Britain.

The National Emblem

The State Emblem of India is a replica of the Sarnath Lion capital of Ashoka, near Varanasi in Uttar Pradesh. It depicts four lions standing back to back and stands for power, courage and confidence.

National Anthem

Jana Gana Mana is the national anthem of India.

National Flower

Lotus

National Tree

Indian banyan

National Animal

Royal Bengal tiger

National Bird

Indian peacock

Find out More

Primary and Secondary Sources

A primary source is information created by someone who was a part of or witnessed the historical event first hand. Primary sources are very important to historians researching events and time periods. Examples of primary sources are letters, emails, filmed interviews and clips, journals and diaries, census statistics, government documents, art and maps (from the time period), the news (both print and film), photographs and maps.

A secondary source is when someone who did not actually witness the event retells the facts that someone else told them. Examples of secondary sources include news (both print and film), interviews, letters, journals and diaries, biographies, textbooks and paraphrased quotations.

Glossary

BUDDHISM: religion based on the teachings of Buddha

CASTE : the social group in which Hindus are born

CLIMATE CHANGE: shift in the planet's weather and climate patterns

CULTURE PRACTICES: beliefs and customs of a society or people

ENDANGERED: when a species is at risk

ETHNIC GROUP: people who share a common culture, language and heritage

HIGHLANDS: mountainous or elevated region

MATCHMAKER: someone who arranges marriages on behalf of the bride and groom's family

MONSOON: season of heavy rain

PLATEAU: large, flat area found in higher regions

RICKSHAW: small passenger vehicle pulled by someone running or riding a bike

SUSTAINABILITY: to support and maintain the environment

TUK TUK: motorised rickshaw

Index